Connected Journeys

PUBLISHED BY
Mkuki na Nyota Publishers Ltd
P. O. Box 4246
Dar es Salaam, Tanzania
www.mkukinanyota.com

© Joanna Skelt, 2014

ISBN 978-9987-08-238-4

Con

For Konya

Thanks to all those who have helped me along this journey and to Dave whose networking led me to this extraordinary publisher.

1. ORIGINAL LANDSCAPE

A landscape of tugs, frigates, cruise and cargo ships
dinghies, speed boats, trawlers
and yachts of all imaginable dimensions
alongside pontoons and docks,
quays accessed by numerous steps and slipways
and those brightly painted boats that trundle up and down
saying the same old thing each day to the same old tourists
who only smile when the sun comes out.

I could sit here all day,
imagining possible escape routes
voyages, nurturing my desire to journey
connect, view things differently
change…

A childhood long spilled
into shallow waves that now carry me to estuaries
flood into creeks, become mud then flood again
yet still retain their beauty.

There is an oldness about things here,
the land, a quiet settledness
cast upon this place
at odds with what must once have been.

Who knows what cultures crossed and traded here?
Who stumbled, bedazzled and afflicted?
Who stood and stared at the strangers disembarking
-like they stare from bridges at the sight of black swans?
Who received the first letter from Alexandria
-and what did it say?
Who tasted ginger for the first time?

I can taste it too: it is still here
amongst the dracaena palms and exotic entrance ways
the cartographic maps shops,
where each new wreck is plotted by hand
on paper coastlines off the Turtle islands
by men who drank with German mercenaries
fighting the Biafran war.

There are old figureheads from packet ships
down narrow streets
saffron cakes and ginger biscuits,
alongside the ethnic shops
that sell statuettes of Yermaya
– goddess of the ocean.

The sea is as much a god here as the old stones
as though everything were tinged,
the way that salt tinges the skin
and makes us move more slowly.

There are relics from old boats
bits of weathered glass and rope
placed like talismans around the gardens
where ageing sailors sit gazing from porches
their huge lives stretched out languidly
across a blue horizon.

And I feel towards this place
like a man must feel towards his wife,
I want to cover her in silk,
venerate and keep her for myself.

2. LOVE SONG TO THE RIVER CAM

Serpentine and ever-so-contentedly-smiling,
you mostly seem to sleep,
yet each single piece of rain, movement of an oar
or swan, so very gently gliding,
momentarily unmakes you.

How quickly you re-smooth yourself
reminds me of those houses
where everything is tidied up
and you are not supposed to make an imprint,
small ripples barely raise you
from your slumber.

What is it you say in the morning
when you part to let the rowers by,
the same ones who from the bridge, at night
appear as a millipede or ancient ship?

Eternal gypsy, do you become attached
to these banks?
What I know of you is never
all you are.

Almost still, you give of yourself
everything, require nothing, ask for nothing
hold no grudge or scars from all the criss-crossing,
spearing and carving up all day
from punt poles and outboard motors.

River, my cat-self wants to try out each spot,
each vantage point.

You steal past me
as a smooth viola, like the thought of coffee,
your skin old hunting boots,
the colour of many-traded guns.

You wear the sun like I wear
these mirror sunglasses, these trees
and houseboats your proud medals and jewels,
each day accompanying me
in and out of town, my chaperone.
I take my pulse from you each morning,
and again at night when returning home,
I stop.

Generations I trace in you,
once I would have washed in you,
fought over you, you would have been
my life blood, water-bearer.

River-god, shape of a bull with human head
– or horse, they painted you,
here, in gentle incarnation, languorous:
lying down, wafted by exotic willows,
hardly caring to move.

Oh river, sacred consolation, rise up!
If I were Arethusa, I would have wanted you
– would have loved you back,

I want to see you in the rain, and after rain,
before the storm, in the snow
and flooding at your banks,
I long to see you emptied out
– your contours.

In your wildest moments
you become to me upturned,
wild liana to the sky, ladder to the heavens,
waterfall, a route to elsewhere, an escape,
make what you will of me,
I, too, am all arteries,
hidden channels and connections.

Oh river, how I love that you are alive
and pass through here!

3. FIRST NIGHT

This is the first night I ever wanted you
and I am in tatters.

The sprawling shadows, ever longer on the heath
the grass -as moist as fell- has overwhelmed me.
I hold my head in my hands.

This is the first night I ever wanted you
with what I do not want as well - which is hardest,
how to conjure rain
when we had slept like deer and woken startled
and estranged
then rediscovered words.
And you asked me why I didn't say.

This is the first night I ever wanted you,
this ordinary night without festivity
where there are no exaggerations
and even you are absent.

What does it matter? The night is cold
and I can remember how it was before you,
so many gestures, tokens, and heights that have now faded
men I once ached over,

and then you with your storytelling and obsessions
the way you ritualise the mundane
with those glazed eyes —so hard to pinpoint
where their brownness ends and white begins-
and a pragmatism that is all worn out by nightfall.
You are only half foreign to me.

All the same, I wonder what the cards would say?
The deities invoked in flame-lit circles,

the charmer with his huge green snake,
the medicine man outside your grandma's house
-and what would she say?
And all the spirits that fill our rooms,
sweep our pathways,
preside over rivers and marketplaces…?

And it occurs to me this very moment
that I love you -without extremes or heights,
like an earthiness, a balance of the scales
the way the earth itself
allows each of us our footsteps.

There are usually mountains
that loom somewhere to steal my sky-line,
to spur me onwards and seduce me
but tonight they cloak the dark like purple silk
and no longer seem like mountains
but roots in the night,
on the first night I wanted you.

4. TODAY IS LIKE

Everything has been drawn
with a fine nib,
in perfect focus.

All things move me.

Even the shadows
pierce me.

This morning is
precise yet soporific
and, lying here, I revel in it,
as if I were the model and this a painting
or scorpion basking
in a sun which tips out colour,
coating everything with gloss.

Above, the sky is thickly painted turquoise blue
and I am sure the ocean, too, is flat today like oil
and closer to its essence.

Near to me, a bird sings
and overtakes, for once,
my own song.

Today, I can imagine how it must feel
to be rooted like a plant
and relish the wind.

Even the outdoor table gives itself up:
the strawberry tablecloth, yellow tea pot
the huge green bowl which, like the day itself, overflows
and I am almost wounded
by the pleasure of it.

5. SITIAN SEA

Morning, outside the mini-market
the sea glances, serpent eyed,
swings like a pocket watch
-or pendulum,
dragging me in.

My window, the sky:
hills no longer hills
but ancient armadillos,
legs outstretched, turned to stone,
the olive trees, tavernas and apartments
like barnacles on the hulls of ships,
-barely noticed, time is measured
so much more slowly here.

This is not Sitian sea
but a million seas
content to travel through,
to seep across my maps
her vicious metal played out
on other shores, Olokun…

Here, flashing yellow in a blink,
a flick of beads,
spume becoming powder-white, to mist
disentangling, disintegrating into wind,
breaking right to left
in furious piano scale
or instant theatre.

By night, Sitia sits in black,
sea melted, treacle-like,
an entirely altered continent
which cancels itself out

into a nothingness, an infinity,
a presence so close to sky
it must run over.

Around the promenade,
palm trees, enamoured of the sea,
collect like groupies, stand splayed,
all given over,
and I wonder, what is this thing,
this sea? This great thick spinning soup,
full of wheels and turning moons?

Somewhere in all this, I have flung my nets,
somewhere in all this, the shapes of things
emerge from waves
like images in flames
when everyone's asleep or drunk on raki,
or wishing for love or loving,
or grieving.

And miles from Sitia too,
landlocked inhabitants trawl and retrawl,
their invisible moorings stretched out,
creaking, each night reaching for sea,
each night an incoming tide
retreating suddenly from opened eyes,
shrinking across ethers
into a dot, into a pixel piece of
Mediterranean, retessellating,
remaking this Sitian morning.

6. URBAN ARRIVAL

A flash of October green and gold
coats my day,
as I cycle, briefly, through the park,
in between the fumes, digits on screens
and dreams I still manage to harbour
in distant ports,
along with the colour turquoise.

Trees. It doesn't matter what they're called,
they are my escape- a palette,
I gorge myself,
investigate every branch, each arm
whose shadow falls, stretching
eel-like, into a precise oil
into which I linger.

Paper, tons and tons of it, piles
I juggle, trickster-like
amidst the continents and words,
the cafes I inhabit, near-religiously
-where I consume,
full of prams and noise,
where the road-side, framed in glass
shines, just occasionally, like a river.

Hats off to them, these urban folk, canal-happy,
accustomed to the hotch-potch, disappearing sky
sliced up, the commotion, thriving on it,
hooked on jazz, how do they do it?
And Carribean Sam, his sweet potatoes
sitting in the window of his shop
like old party streamers -- no doubt smiling,
but what has he done
with the sea?

And this whole city thing,
everything sown together -me even,
into a night mesh, all appearing joined up,
breaks jaggedly into a jigsaw of days, layers,
lines and crimsons, metal snakes,
that I rattle, unravel then throw
into my sleep like stones whose ripples settle,
somewhere becoming still.

And there I am–miraculously,
another miniscule rectangle, a piece or dot
in this colossal cog, driving ever on and on...

7. ON BEING IN FREETOWN

Now wondering if I was there at all
arriving and departing, as I did,
through thunder, frantic theatre
sky flashing faster than
our crazy airplane,
crimson clouds lit spectacularly
like frozen lava.

How are we expected to simply carry on
when we have seen such things?
How can I walk unflinchingly along Alcester road
and slot back in, when last Monday
I sat up there, maps moving underneath me
as I watched on screen?

I cannot make sense
of these lines of terraced houses,
I want to make rubble of them
recreate the red dust streets
then use the broken bits – frames, planks
to bang together shacks
but I cannot piece it,
cannot make sense of the patchwork
there is now.

In part, I live on still in Lumley,
daily I traverse Wilkinson road,
and, like a prisoner exercising memory,
investigate each road I missed,
re-remember houses.

I am struck, altered even,
by the extreme exuberance
of the flamboyant trees – flame red,

the fat oval leaves of the tree
that no one knew the name for
-'whit man's groundnut' or giant bay?
which stood squat, and spinach green
rapt beyond us
in the switch to rain.

And between the winding muezzin,
whir and unwhirring of fans,
near where the car, in half an hour,
became a rail for selling clothes
-donated once as aid,
between the hard-angled jazzing of streets
the hotch-potch, ramshackle, broken jigsaws
jagged glass on the walls, through this montage,
light reflected, fired back and forth
the haze, barrage, in this kaleidoscopic-snapshot,
time seemed to stop, to hang there,
as I negotiated routes, moorings
held onto lines thrown to me in books
and explanations, resonances,
my stranger's eyes, remembering 1997,
last November, overlaying outlines I already knew
to form a stronger thread.

And Freetown bears it, grins
names itself on walls to stop itself undoing
- to keep itself sown,
and like an old Mercedes
welded, overfilled, it swaggers
ragamuffin-like, a marching band
blowing its crumpled trumpet,
chasing its devils from the graveyards,
its women walking tall their baskets
still-lifes of coconuts and fried plantain,
of plastic water bottles, each one a moving

chandelier on top of zig-zag braids
and gara-dyed dresses.

Meanwhile Kru town festers,
Celtel-red, ablaze with Emerson,
eyes black, slow-spinning
peer back, at my white woman's
thirty-eight-ness
as another oddity, and old
in a country that is *so* young
yet seen so much.

And this place slowly seeps
into the wood of me, my grain,
my body pushed up to an edge
humbled by the miles
and years, the crossing points
that brought me here,
now folded into me,
so much so the sky,
the clouds framed by trees,
opening along the A14,
I redraw into lines of blue
white, green, into a flag
through which I reinhabit,
revisit Freetown again.

8. ENGLISH EYES IN SIERRA LEONE

Batiq-clad, in Man United shirts
they climb Spur Road,
Temnes, Mendes, Lokos,
Limbas with scars, Fulahs..
their burdens head-high:
      eggs resting impossibly
      on cardboard waves,
      charcoal awaiting the inevitable fire
      stacked in tiers, balanced Pisa-like
      against my straight, known world
      of handbags and back packs.

How can a street
contain so many cracks
to slip through,
so many languages and threads
to unravel?

I cannot even begin
to read this street,
streaming, one moment
clogging the next,
tessellating, retesselating
in the blink-back of my English eyes
as the tired unmoving
silhouettes, freeze-framed
and shading under trees,
gaze through layers,
beyond the location,
beyond the lifetimes.

I wonder am I too thin
too unrooted for all this?

Freetown: here homes are places
I no longer have access to,
a glimpse only, and taxi drivers
want to slaughter goat for me,
no – for an English address,
everyone wants to be my friend.
I guard my heart, keep space
for elsewhere,
retain my seemingly luxurious
belief in love, and my home
wedged into an Asian world
-and English otherness,
at best it is relationships,
easinesses, the freedom to be
left alone when I walk to the shop
to buy milk or a newspaper. To blend.

I cast these thoughts
across landscapes passing from a car
as the window breeze
becomes a welcome fan,
loosens my preoccupation with heat
and I catch back my thoughts
stich them, find meaning, solidity
in the rope-knot feeling of them
holding together the rungs
of my makeshift bridge.

I write these words, as the radio
speaks in tongues, shrieks and screams
works itself tornado-style, and I dream
of a glorious unwinding
in that net of night-time
which liberates,
unmakes my Englishness
unmakes this African-ness, this pen,

continuing to drum up,
document, to put its nib on this page,
at this compass point, in this place, city,
country, continent, spinning supercontinent
to write out what these days are
what these eyes have seen…

9. IN GOD WE TRUST

Proclaims the poda poda
slamming into Charlotte Street
the waiting hoards stampeding,
blinded with dust, rushing for seats,
wrapped in sweat which drips, slips
and ticks on through hours
sinking into a history
no one cares to capture.

Expert elbows force their way
to sit shoulder-locked, clutching dirty
hand to dirty bag, the occasional foreigner
and thief squeezed into the mix of jeans
and Africana, all gulping for the air
which refuses to enter through the window gap,
passengers sending out for solace through SMS
chatting on mobile phones, connected,
disconnected, sweat ticking still,
everyone forced witnesses
to this theatre.

I wonder where everyone is going,
ever shunting along these broken roads
in a city stumbling without light,
engines sellotaped together by drivers
hooked on jamba, devoted to Manchester United,
their country spilt around them, ever moulded,
ridden over, mined, made into a playground
for NGOs and temporarily 'rich' men
just back from Peckham and Maryland?

Inside the poda poda, the passengers
make their peace and wars
inside themselves, within the solace

of skins and minds, recalling
an unanswered call to prayer,
or pastor bellowing his discontent,
a wife or mistress merging with a woman
from a film who sold her soul -or found it after all,
others recalling no words at all,
given in to blankness -a kind of gateway,
trusting that God will deliver them home,
that everything is for a purpose
and this, too, will pass.

Meanwhile jeeps trundle past, near empty,
equally slow, air conditioning burning up
the petrol (cut with palm oil), trailing fat fumes
along streets already choked
with cooking smoke and the fuming
of unmoving travellers,
their wants out of reach, suspended,
threaded as they are into Aberdeen road
on Wednesday 19th November, 2008
the city gloriously dysfunctional around them,
each one in their own way contributing,
adding to the burden.

It must look a picture
from the helicopter overhead
spinning its ex-pats and middle classes
across the ether into airport land,
a serpent sleeping on the way to Lumley,
its extraordinary skin - a jig-map of
car shapes, headlights, and the half-haze
of kerosene flames,
up there you might imagine
you could see innumerable lines
flung outward to all the cities, landscapes
and faces linked to people sitting stationery

on their journey home, a scattered web,
or ladder. Perhaps it resembles hope?

And each day Freetown's inhabitants
are made in this, pass from calendar
to calendar, growing here,
intertwined in this ritual of traffic
halting nightly, holding them in its grasp
subject to the shifting shapes
the patterns repeated, ingrained, imprinted
on the marble cracks of eyes and slow wrinkling
of so many desperate, happy
or resigned lives.

10. SOWN-TOGETHER TREES

What has been
so very carefully
stitched together,
unravels
along the airplane route
London, Brussels
Abidjan, Accra
a red ribbon trailing
across the TV screen
mirroring the globe
we thunder over.

Countries pushed together
crowded, sleeping
as recent strangers sleep,
harbouring in each other's warmth
across this wilderness
or no man's land,
fitting next to one another,
puzzle-like, a patchwork,
sown-together, made…

Nations, identities and languages
overlaid on top of soil and sand,
temporarily suspended,
the passengers uprooted -like moving trees,
trying to read, to divine futures
amongst the ether and the flash
of nameless settlements
(and they, below, interpreting
our shadow and our roar)
as if this movement were a transit
to a new beginning, all of us
wrenched.

It is beyond us, this journey
from heaven to heaven,
plunging through clouds
into unknown continents,
leaving us open, bare
our world momentarily un-made,
borders and boundaries
disintegrating into threads,
the branches, roots
and very leaves of us
I see now are merely
sown-together.

11. TO THE SHOE SELLERS AT CIRCLE

Forgotten queens, ill-illuminated
by kerosene, they peddle dreams:
ladies shoes laid in grids across the ground,
high heels – shining red and gold, strappy sandals,
platform wedges in champagne leather
evoking dim-lit clubs and nollywood escapes,
while across the colossal traffic roundabout
distorted highlife music plays …

I wonder who wore these shoes before
who circled and swayed to the endless cover songs
played by musicians later traipsing
past these forgotten queens to Picadilly's
red-eyed worlds? Trumpet players
drinking Star beer, dreaming of stardom
in the diamond dazzling dizziness of 3am,
conjuring angels from the prostitutes
who are ruffled now -themselves lost queens –
smiles slipped away, teetering on 4 inch stilettos,
blind to the neverending circling,
everything returning here like debris
swept into a corner, spinning, a circling
vortex or faultline.

The shoe sellers, on nightly vigil, see it all,
keep their flames alive miraculously in the rain
amidst the stench and splash, the roundabout
clogged with wishes for redirection,
soothed by the push and pull,
the ever-circling ever-present dust, fumes,
charcoal and cheap perfumes,
the passing drum beat of footsteps and click of
poor man's charliewatte,
each time around this place, ever more tied in
bound in, wound up, wound in with what this city is.

I wonder who will buy shoes here at this hour
in the rain and darkness, in the sluggish air
at such a juncture? Each shoe laid out
independently as though one shoe
could still offer one small step to the glamour
of another world, an option to walk away
from this, from the sodden orphans
and itinerants on the flyover barely asleep
on a tiny bag of their possessions,
nearly trodden on by the passing strangers
criss-crossing and ever-circling through this
crossroads, hub, this interchange
tended by so many forgotten queens.

12. TREE BLOW

Our ritual, post night-cap -Herb Afrik
to stop near dawn by the outdoor table
even the wind blowing freely now
through unkempt palms.

Around us, everyone asleep for once
and we, slower at this hour
giving in to what all hearts want now
the simple yet extraordinary
geography of kisses
matched only by the final stop
at home
where there are still
hours to pass till morning.

13. HIGHER

It is a high thing, that tugs
unexpectedly, the magpie for once
with mate, the southern hemisphere
glare of a once-familiar yellow shrub,
the blackbird, high up, weaving
his invisible song.

Outside my door, the spindly cherry tree
has managed blossom, manages
to undo me, as I return home
twilight-drunk, its presence
somehow heightened, imbued
as if inner-lit.

It climbs in through tentatively-opened
windows, through a crack, spills out
as laughter in houses that have been dark
and zipped all winter.

It is the chord of blues, the sea
here now, lake-like, islands sleeping
pre-historically as the pine trees gather
by the shore the way old men gather
in shady cafes by the market square,
sitting, as my grandpa sat
mesmerised by the songthrushes
in his garden.

It is the shabby, sequined city,
gazing up to stars, me gazing down
both of us pliable, opened up
struck with something higher
than what or who it is we are.

It is the bud, the seed, the egg,
the deepening thread of friendship
sown into us, underneath us
like the foundations of houses
holding us there, in these lives
shifting startlingly around us
like winds, it is the sap,
the single shoot pushing out of
farrow land, beyond the deadwood,
the pain, the violence of upheavals,
the lonelinesses.

Higher than me, than flight
than the late quartet in C
as if written in my own key,
higher than the meeting cross of a kiss,
the kiss itself inseparable from ether.

14. COPPER BEECH TREE

Winter mornings, the jazziness
of waking, eyes-half closed
to the negative flash of white tree
through black air...

A cross-word, maze, calendar
of roots, entangled limbs, of tributaries,
one branch becoming many,
becoming one, a tangle of fires
and destinies, I ascend, descend,
scour for clues over mugs of tea
from my tiny attic kitchen.

Long pent up, the copper beech
carries itself through winter
like a wiry cat -haunches up,
clenched, every single ounce
of old sun re-routed,
driving its inner factory.

Each morning, bleary-eyed
from behind my curtains
age-old, frozen messengers,
the colour of Somali dust
cluster, await my audience.

I missed the precise moment
the new leaves eased out,
bound up, packed in layers
like intricate cigars learning
to unravel, missed too
when they revealed themselves
not green but red -near purple,
beetle-backed, in armour,

polished by the rain, then drying
to a rattle, an ornate outdoor screen,
forming the pattern of my days.

15. MOTOROLA LOVE

A line flung over Niger, Mali,
Morocco and Marseille
on Saturday, in the car park
by the Old Rep, Birmingham,
a blue sharpness already
searing my day's snake longing.

One word, *Otidin?* replaces
the funky jangle of my
super skinny Motorola
and, flooded blue, we speak
in ether, he in hot, chaotic
city, where the gig tonight,
says someone by the name
of Bright, is..
then our echoes
break into the world's crackle
-another faulty satellite above
the desert, another top up card.

'Call Ended', I wind my way
Blue Monk tapping from eons,
down ramps I fire my song and
striving over, into a now
neon city opened out in front
of me, my phone's silver
smooth flash busy hurtling
mercurial rivers, sits quietly
against my skin as near to me
as a lover's hand.

16. LUNCHTIME CONCERT, EDGBASTON

I can anchor here,
an hour, more even,
feel myself malleable
silken.

It is not what it *is*
that plays,
instead, from velvet chair
I give myself to music,
waiting for an opening,
a resonance or moment,
when I can conjure
the cliff path to Sennan Cove,
the presence
of an horizon only.

Cast away from line on line,
from grids of cars
compressed, imprinted, as if a filter
or grey mosaic,
through beaten clouds,
from red-brick home on home
-all temporary junctures of a life-time,
cast momentarily
from the swirl of loving.

Here, through looping,
curving song, thread of wind
I free my soul
across the water.

The precise point
of a minor note, sung high
into an inner arc,

transforms to tip of wave,
stills to desert contour
cut the colour of sky.

At this very point
-suspended beyond time in me,
the shape this sound makes
no longer desert wave
but body turned towards me
in the night,
a perfect border, outline, line
now loosens to ropes
that I can fling, hold, coil…

And all that matters is this line
this height, these loosened
ropes, my spirit out there
intimately connected with waves
as if a gull soaring from a rock,
its feathers intricately woven
by tiny strings, which play, spread,
and seep their colours,

and all the while
my shadow mirrored across the sea
dispersed, almost absorbed by it.

17. CHARLIE

I like the way your hands
delve, almost thoughtlessly,
to pull out chords
each one unexpected,
elemental…like this.

I wonder if they are not hands
at all, but long thin wands
carved mischievously
by a deity
presiding over song?

I like the way your keyboard
seemed to play itself,
seep into my rhythms
while I slept,
and how we tore sleep
from night's pages
in hot strips,
then rearranged them
into our own
music in the morning.

I like, too, the way our hands
make quiet jazz
and tie it all in,
-what it is we call
this world we live in now,
its silver river moving
like mercury between us,
-even across continents,
who knows where we are headed now?

And you know, Charlie,
I conjure black and white piano keys
in classrooms and I love it
when the children
start to see the music in magpies
and in the many-coloured streets
they themselves give colour to.

I love it all,
the way the square edges
of keys fall into curves
that I refind in the curlicues
and scrolls of the gabled houses
where I live, which come alive
and sing to me,
which I breathe in,
then blow out through my saxophone
in S shapes when I get home
sending them southwards…

18. PHOENIX MASQUERADE

a jazz poem in praise of the saxophone

A bird mask on the wall
lit by flame, flashes then frees itself
zig-zags across the stage
flies and soars, up and down
through loops of sound –jijikas,
a spirit moving within the song,
across it, under it, adjacent to it
diving, whirling, squealing out a bent high D
as if cast out as a line or rope,
a bridge between
the people and their soul,
playing mischievously with each instrument,
drunk, flying when it wants to,
bursting into fire, dying when it wants to
then resurrecting,
back in form again,
to ground.

Shapeshifter, golden bird
sits back, brooding, joins in,
adds its own voice to the song,
flights, pleads, seduces, growls and weeps,
furiously climbs scales, cutting out blue notes
repeating and repeating, jumping over hurdles,
a masquerade ripping up the town.

Shaman, acrobat, wildly running up and down,
spirit free, lassoing, stopping, starting,
not knowing what or where
becoming something else –desire or pain,
through ether, rising high, a liquid sun
reduced to glint, to essence, gold,

then solid, becoming silent again,
a bird mask on the wall.

19. TRAVEL SICKNESS

I arrive back in a daze of maps
of Libyan desert, Acrra receding orange-gold
my winged-self up there somewhere still.

Crossing London my magnet slants,
both sick and heavy at the same time,
my organs shifted, I cannot readjust,
am out of kilter, oriented elsewhere.

For seven days I clamber through
as if through smoke, eyes stinging,
wrenched, cast open, clutching at clocks
and phones, all the while praying for new
life… Books, news, visits to my friends,
capturing the transitory beauty of leaves,
quiver in the corner at the weight of this.
Of this? What else is there now?

The criss-crossing I have done
cannot be uncrossed now. The consequences
of traversing continents play through me
in songs that stop, unfinished
and I can only sit, absorb, saturate,
feel through air to piece myself together,
reach for scales to climb in crazy ladders
searching for an outlet or wings again.

Cut alone, flailing, a solitary boat
moored at the wrong harbour, waiting for wind,
for a sign, for God, I don't know.
I cannot believe the force of it, the overlaying
across all else as if an awful lens,
and meanwhile in Birmingham
it rains and rains when only days and nights ago

it rained so strongly that we stayed inside
and it was no longer each other's water
but the rain itself we seemed to share.

Even the startling appearance of the sun
serves only to heighten and hone
my glass-felt realisation
that this life is over, it abandoned me
while I was living elsewhere, loving elsewhere.
I have to try hard to remember myself.

20. LAKES

Day four, or maybe five, and sleep?
I could bite into it, open mouthed,
suck it all in, gulps of it,
each starry morsel spinning into me
like morphine or first milk,
healing these aching arches
still flashing with surgical lights,
the last eight months [and more] coiled, winding and
unwinding
around the corridors of the Women's Hospital
like a spirit running to catch up
when it has flown so far.

God, how I prayed along those corridors
sat there, at 20 weeks, retracing my steps, post Africa
willing him or (as I know now) her, to come,
closed my eyes at the ultrasound:
just tell me everything's OK is all I said.
Later, the impossibility of tracing the outline
of my child from a black and white glimpse
of a world within, and from that outline
divining an essence, a soul even?

How I willed the weeks to pass -and on,
remoulded myself,
dressed my shape in different cloth
until, finally, that last week,
last three days - those corridors again,
Mandy's cheese scones and cans of Guinness
smuggled onto Ward 3, stored beside
the galloping heart machine – with its paper zig-zags
endlessly printing out the evidence of inner life.

Then a crazy 3am, downstairs, *behind* the corridors
to rooms- the realm of gods
inhabited by hands and bleeps, the panic of machines
awash with sobs and flesh, where hours in,
eventually I succumbed, was opened
shivering and numb amidst voices, brightness
and sky-blue medical scrubs
to first glimpse of *a* girl, weenie, bundle-rapped,
her skin to mine, tears chasing after tears, tumbling over,
my entire self leaking, spilled, a lake
all of it bound with her, pure connection,
love is too tame a word. It is liquid now, raw form.

And noon today, along the corridors of the hospital again,
this time accomplice to what lies behind,
I traipse wounded, undone, altered
the blue metal stitches pulled out from me,
the car seat in grandpa's hands, inside my little daughter,
her miniscule shoots of hair already criss-crossed with kisses
her butterfly breaths, -each one, miraculous- drain and then
replenish
the lakes new born in me.

21. IT SNOWS IN BIRMINGHAM

From Bearwood to Shard End, Sparkhill to Lozells
from Erdington to Frankley, it snows.

It snows on new mothers and disgruntled postmen
freezing on bikes, up since 5,
on the long-term unemployed and policemen
-both snowball-ready- and on lawyers in sharp suits alike.

It snows on the Somali boy gazing for the first time
on a world made white not by people but by snowflakes
which he later draws in school, hangs up at home
as a happy reminder – as art in life,
and on the little girl with spotted Wellingtons
whose snowman sports an organic nose.

It snows on in lives hardened by shopping for Christmases
which rarely come, and lives angled unknowingly by the daily
panorama of tower blocks and trunk roads.

From Smethwick to Solihull, a city altered, frosted,
black trees re-stencilled white, underpinned by snowdrops,
and it is hard not to believe in some kind of magic
when, to cap it all, the sun comes out.

Only occasionally does it snow like this,
through the red brick walls working its way slowly into rooms
thawing still more slowly into the thick of us –into souls
that for once float freely with the miraculousness of things.

Rarely does it snow so much, it seeps through cracks on roads
into the drains and dregs of Birmingham,
the phoenix fire-cold touch of snow absolving misdemeanours done,
seeps beyond again past the grime, its white blaze
penetrating what this city is, at its heart, the idea of itself:

people spun from ether, living side by side,
made better by the criss-cross interactions,
making meaning, making music from it all,
sharing the same colleges and hospitals, the same cinemas
and skylines, the same parks (now inhabited by sledges and
sleighs)
living in the medley, amidst the shapes and squares, the lines
ever making patterns.
A city life forgotten in the flash of commerce and commotion
driving ever forward, the weather in its usual grey guise
passing unspectacularly, egging us on, blinkered.

But today it is snowing from Shirley to Moseley to Oldbury
and it keeps on snowing, holding us –citizen and city,
blackbird and school (marooned today in the whiteness all
around),
– enthralled in its unexpected spell.

22. TWILIGHT

It isn't midnight, 3am but twilight
which sings the deepest song,
imbues the cityscape with unexpected glow
as veils change, there is only thin veneer
and we sense our world as if through flames,
the city's hour of divination
when today, history and tomorrow
fuse into a golden slur
and everything seems possible.

Twilight across Birmingham
so many grades of it that swirl then settle
on the swanky new apartment blocks
whose balconies look back at you
as a coloured dot, pixellated
a digital flash, a speck
or a piece of a mosaic,
as city wallpaper for Brindley place,
for the slices of staccato high rise,
frozen, chiselled, chopped,
whose lines blur
becoming slower – *rallentando*
as the day runs out
and twilight asserts itself.

Edgbaston reservoir, in a finger snap
the sky takes charge,
overshadows the empty spires
turned silhouettes, overshadowed by
the bronzing, dazzling windows
of ramatazzic tower blocks
which at 9pm glare sultry and flamenco like
in the flashing gold,
all around, the water

chopped into tumbling hexagons,
a sea of tessellating grey mirrors,
the tower blocks
now mirrored checkerboards
as the sun strikes its ancient message
through the threaded lines and links.

And from the bank, a lone man stands
chanting to the gods, Augusta, to ancestors,
to his own self, swirling, lassoing, looping,
casting out ropes reaching for the sky,
amidst the tin percussion of halyards chinking on masts,
the flap and slam of the sails as the booms swing over,
the hollering of helmsman to crew,
all this song blown in wild tangents over blocks
broken into pieces that echo their way
to Hagley road, to Five Ways roundabout
spin, become another grain or glint of sound
picked up by someone stuck in traffic
later whistled, tapped out in a bar
where someone plays a clarinet and blows it back
now fused into something else, into jazz........

In the same bar one of the sailors from the reservoir
feels a resonance, taps his toe, so much moving in him
seemingly unknown, his *own* sea
governed by its own weathers, clocks,
springs and compasses......

It isn't midnight, 3am but twilight
which sings the deepest song.

23. LETTER TO A FATHER

Who has not lived up to his name.
I send this due south -as the swifts fly
visa-less, seeking out your sun.

Perhaps these swifts will bring you word
or more likely, unbeknownst, you may hear their song
sitting in your morning dream,
in what the puzzle makers carved out as Africa.

I send this message-in-a-bottle
from my orange room, glimpse of terraced rooftop,
TV aerials where, through the sometimes blue,
a rook or magpie perches: "hello birdie" our daughter cries.
How can you not have touched her skin
already wrapped in stars?

Charlie, I am older, wiser and more foolish
than ever it would seem
but our child sleeps in the other room
and is full of spark and flash of synapse.

Late at night in Tree Blow,
infinitesimal breeze loosening our chords,
the couple at the bar, do you remember them?
She so full, an entire moon stretched inside her
husband standing by, both mute, struck by her light
and the imminent arrival…

You never saw me like this, moon-struck and all given over.
And now no little dress, no token arrives at all, at all.
And so I send this to you on transparent wings,
in soliloquy, through the ether,
for I am mother, the house, the rock.

You, who made with me, in Bubiashie
a girl, more beautiful than lake and sea,
a gift, result of compass point, of music...

24. URBAN GAMES

From Sparkhill to Solihull,
rips of sunlight
race from bumper to wheel trim
spin then die in diamond flashes
echoing an ancient swordplay,
as we race and weave our way
over the din on din of stereos
past the stop, start, beep, screech, amber
the 'TO LET' signs, past the colossal superstores
–selling beds and dreams, and the showrooms
which begin to glitter as the city unravels,
and, at the back of our traffic-tired eyes, a torch,
a flame urging us on, sharing the one goal
of moving forward.

Fifteen minutes later, the gym,
running, rowing, plugged into MP3s, SKY news,
reality TV shows, children squealing
in the café below, everything echoing
over loud speakers which pour out Heart FM
as we stare at the swimming pool
where, twenty minutes later,
the shock of turquoise brings us closer
to something higher, that Olympian blue…

Maybe it is this that drives us on
back through the stop, start, beep, screech, amber
to our living rooms, sofas, to Wimbledon
on wide screen, or Villa Park, gymnastics
and, again, that higher blue
threading us into other cities, lands,
supporters glued to makeshift screens
in Kamayama, Adabraka or Eileen Road
where the window cleaner on the ladder,

headphones on, is tuned to England at Edgbaston
he, too, bearing a torch.

25. MOSAIC HEART

I gather them together
shards

the best of my relationships
exquisitely reduced down
into turquoises, fuchsias

kaleidoscopic essences
which flash – diamanté like
with memory and charge
as if the connection - the very *kernel* of it
were captured here, still flowing

precious shards
fragments of broken bridges
bricks from abandoned altars

the zebra stripe
of fingers intertwined

golden threads
once chasing, tying, rooted down
now embroider this tapestry

stencilled too with remembered wings

and so this Valentine
I shun the roses, the scarlet hearts
and piece together
this mosaic.

26. LITTLE BOY HOMS

We lost Marie Colvin too,
the journalist who told us
only days before
of your loss:
a little boy, just two years old,
another casualty in the craziness.

Syria imploding around you,
the land that gave you life
has changed its mind.

And what can I do, driving
through Stirchley, Birmingham
late, to collect my two year old
images of you erupting
through the airwaves?

I cannot repeat what Marie
Colvin told us, how she watched
you go, like so many other
innocents in the wars I study:
Sierra Leone, Liberia,
the list goes on…

All of it a damning indictment
of our times, of ourselves,
me, too, sitting here
planning tomorrow's tasks, blinkers on,
desperately changing channels
to stop the visions of you
from seeping in.
What kind of Gods, of Allahs
and international organisations
have we forged that allow such acts

to go past almost unflinchingly
in our daily lives?

Each one of us spun like dice
across continents we carve
into countries, religions, factions.

Little boy from Homs
perhaps the Christians were right,
that Eve's apple released
our serpents: tyranny, weapons, hate,
which flash out their lightning tongues
and take the best from us.

Little boy Homs
-and all those you have joined,
may we learn to be more worthy of you
the next time that you come.

27. THE SWIFTS OF EILEEN ROAD

Using only leaves and bits of twig,
scrunched up sweet papers, feathers and petals,
the swifts build nests
glued together with saliva
year on year, under the eaves of our houses.

These boomerang-like birds
glide at dusk and dawn in near formation
over our higgledy-piggledy street
with its haphazard tessellations of transit vans,
skips and rubbish left out in the wrong bags,
where the kids once from Limerick, Yemen and
Pakistan zig-zag across the street, shrieking,
their lives permanently linked via satellite
to other countries and continents, climates, social codes
where somehow we jumble in,
and Rudy comes out each day on his way to Aldi
-eyes Barbadian blue,
and the polish couple come out once a week
to water their pansies and get the taxi to hospital,
above us all, the sweep and circle of black crescents
temporarily painting our sky.

All the way from Africa they come, these flying anchors
to fledge their young from the eaves of our houses each summer,
hidden from our eyes: first eggs, then tiny beaks open
squealing for moths and midges, ladybirds
hoovered up -mid-air- by their slick, sky-skating parents
who zoom back to nests, kamikaze-like,
their elegant bat-like silhouettes
disappearing, suddenly, as if a magic act.

I so much want these swifts to come each year,
to bring their swirling news of other climes,
their journey made beyond the politics,
eating, sleeping, mating miraculously on the wing,
accepting of it all, this crazy carved up globe
as the burka comes, recession hits, the pool closes, schools fail,
whether DR Congo's at war or peace, despite Afghanistan
still they come, their radar over sea and land
through Mozambique, Zimbabwe, to England, Sparkhill and
Eileen road
like magnets they are pulled
navigating on a memory of stars
to rear their young under the eaves of our houses.

28. BIRMINGHAM GOLD

On Wednesday, in the middle of this hot-potch
city as if built by scattered lego blocks,
outside Symphony Hall, by the Rep
and the new library, its swirly metal chinks
as yet untested, without pulse, its circles of worlds on worlds
an ideal for now, a mosaic in the mind of a distant architect,
in the space where sometimes a wheel or ice skate spins
a temporary marquee…

Inside all manner, colour and shape
of seventeen year-olds, clad in giant bling:
trombones, trumpets and super-massive saxophones
blowing their burgeoning hearts out and over lunch breaks
and the narrow boats sleeping picturesquely by the canal side
café,
over the A38 chugging snake-like underneath,
its vast army of machines carrying this music
like aid to every quarter.

This city where kids are spun together
homes flung across the globe, daily criss-crossing
classrooms, cleavages and the jangle of not-so-beautiful-streets,
out of all this, a youth orchestra, sounds entwined,
the spangle and glimmer of instruments
momentarily chiming with July's first rays,
threading together the city's seams
into molten gold.

29. WE ARE ENGLAND

Commissioned to welcome the Queen's Baton Relay to Birmingham, UK on 2 June 2014

For two hundred and eighty-eight days,
baton-bearers across the globe - in heat, rain or cold,
have proudly clutched and carried
the Queen's message and a love of sport
on the way to Glasgow for the Games,
as I write this, the baton's more than fifteen hundred miles away in Malta
on route next to Gibraltar,
it has been paraded by bicycle along Lumley beach in Freetown,
and trumpeted in Accra, it has zoomed through Cameroon,
Tanzania, St Kitts, Guyana…
Leaving in its wake a swirl of goodwill across the commonwealth,
resolutions to get fit, aim higher, strive,
and now the baton is here in the heart of England, Birmingham
stencilled with fingerprints
and memories of handshakes and smiles
picked up along the way.

This global journey is re-enacted daily in our city
as new arrivals are plugged into an A to Z
of avenues and offices, shops
gyms and red brick swimming pools,
our many-coloured selves mixing in,
creating a panorama of domes, archways, minarets and spires
a worldly mosaic which animates pre-rush hour
as walkers, runners and cyclists
emerge, move and breathe across Birmingham's green spaces
threaded like ribbons tying us together,
linking our urban lives with trees and sky.

In Ward End Park, ladies –once from Dadyal and Rawalpindi,
shuffle, power walk and run, their many shapes,
swathed in fuchsia, crimson,
scarves bellowing in the late spring breeze,
at the same time early bird swimmers dart up and down
the city's pools like sleek trained fish
and shy kids with packed lunches and plimsolls
arrive for the first time at summer Sports Academies,
at the university athletics track, eager students practice hurdles
and triple jump spurred on by the enduring energy
of Usain Bolt who once trained there,
while all over, busy workers squeeze Zumba,
Bodypump and Combat classes
into already squeezed schedules.

From Aston Villa to cricket at Edgbaston,
Judo to lawn tennis and gymnastics,
our vein of sport runs deep,
as we connect to something higher, exercise, compete,
feel free and energised, engaged,
feel connected – a part of this land,
joined to something bigger: from Birmingham
to Team England, unity under one flag,
one blood pumping across cultures and divides .
– red like these flowers planted in celebration and reminder.

The commonwealth baton brings a unique blessing
guides us to find our own path to sport,
deepens the threads between us
as we identify with others –volunteer coaches
in Belize, Bahamas – just like us,
and support teams which transport us
beyond our petty squabbles and preoccupations
back to what it is which makes us human
and feel alive!
We are *all* England, standing here

on this June day awaiting the baton,
adding our own energy and connectedness
to the message from the Queen,
and sport makes the best of us, of flags,
the red and white of England's
not a cross but an intersection – where we all meet
and come together, like today
to wish the England Team
every success at the Glasgow games.

30. WORDS AND WORLDS

Commissioned for Unesco International Mother Language Day on 21 February 2014

Words
open worlds to me.

Words crammed into rows of books
in libraries bringing characters alive,
histories filed away
under veil of spine and bright blue cover,
dilapidated, thumbed and scribbled in
or magiced to my mobile phone,
all as enticing as a world map.

The cogs of my eyes, mind
and spirit fire,
finding meaning in the 'a's and 'g's,
I am at once home
and elsewhere...

Somalia: through a veil
eye to eye with teenage boys -turned big men,
loose cannons, loitering at the corner
of a Mogadishian street I need to cross,
hired for protection, paid in Khat,
eyes anaesthetised yet piercing,
searching out a fault in me
as though this were a jest,
each page I turn their education slips away,
life expectations count down.

Sierra Leone: the Portuguese face
of a dilapidated, corrugated Kissy Road,
through Freetown's writers

I feel how it must feel
to have survived the end of war,
to be exhausted, extremely free
and yet tormented, trying to suppress
the images of amputation,
which appear like a sudden mugging
in the scarlet song of the flamboyant tree.

Turkey: I whirl with Konya's
dervishes, summoning jinns,
recognise the way each one of us
divines our story from the past,
from the rivers and the winds,
from the symbols where we find ourselves
on this crazy spinning earth.

Through film, I watch Mandela's walk
to freedom, and it makes me
want to order every ounce of energy
to live a better life.

All this transmitted
through my native English language
whose words are everywhere,
on road signs: 'Dog Pool Lane, Cecil Road, B29'
adverts, on buses,

there are sea-side place names like Bognor Regis
painted above the doors of terraced houses
whose million multifarious rooms,
are tied together, interlaced,
jumbled with other cities, villages
and mother tongues
– from English to Bengali
Punjabi, Polish
to Twi, Yoruba and Mandarin…

whose lilt and intonation
clicks, tuts and tumbling laughs
seep through the red brick
like the smell of curry into the living room,
into my very language
which is everyone's now,
ever stretched, made brighter
yet on returning home
I realise I must turn
to English --and only English--
for my private world too.

I find myself recording this,
write it out by hand as small marks,
then read and savour the pages
imprinted, tattooed with ink,
the imagination reproduced
into a visible, tangible item
sent by hand, by digital sky
a route, beyond the borders,
to the very heart of us,
which brings us closer,
our world more into focus.

Words
open worlds to me.

31. CONNECTED JOURNEYS

Commissioned for National Holocaust Memorial Day in Birmingham, UK, January 25, 2014

The great wheel turns
into 2014, another archway
and races on…
Each new year we stop, link hands
sweep the past aside
as if it were easy to rejuvenate,
rebuild, reinvent ourselves
as if it were easy
to forgive.

And here at the centre point of this country
we stand,
the places and people we love
so deeply sown within,
our stories passed down, carried,
at times clenched, like a hard stone,
or sustained as a minor chord by the lonely Croat
whose visions of pines and turquoise
overlay the Digbeth rush hour,
to get back to something pure
before the beauty was polluted, families torn.

I shut my eyes and from these streets
acknowledge the city's faultlines, its cracks,
a world in miniscule:
resentments of the corner shop
without alcohol or English news,
the covering (or exposure) of bare flesh,
objections to adornments, habits
the privileges of wealth and class, of colour even.

From the news streams of global Jihad
to its ramifications in Sparkhill,
mistrust and misunderstanding
neighbours living side by side
but as if epochs away,
from thread of dislike, jealousy
to the spiralling of tribe against tribe,
a daily diet of myth and superstition
passed down, the consequences multiplied ever on.

Here, around us, there are men, women -aged and young,
nursing the remnants of apartheid,
black (and white) people, hearts forever dented
by the abomination of slavery,
tormented by hangings in cotton fields,
our ancestries in feint or fierce way connected
as victims, perpetrators and for failing to act
against the orchestration of mass murders:
the culling of human beings
into pits – their jewellery scavenged
from the sludge of slaughtered skin
Auschwitz, Srebrenica, Kigali, Darfur,
even this city once colluded
in the making of slave chains and armaments.
Amongst us too, are strangers
for whom the terror of their journey
is etched, indecipherably, as a cruel map on their faces,
and men, who barely older than boys
carved out the rounded bellies of women
then watched their two-times dying eyes.
Of course, there are explanations, academic studies
but the taking of even one life
utterly desecrates the miracle of birth and motherhood.

Yet here too, in the very same place
dwell Palestinians and Jews

side by side -the Jewish school is full of Muslim children,
there are Sunni and Shia
and somewhere in the dense fabric of Small Heath,
Sparkbrook or Smethwick
live Hutus…and somewhere Tutsis too,
there are Sudanese
and Somalis with dreams of recreating Mogadishu
schooling their children in English
alongside Pakistanis, Poles, Jamaicans,
Zimbabweans and Chinese.

Each December inhabitants from every creed
and quarter marvel at the German market
all of us making what we can of it, of this time,
our mixed race, mixed heritage children
a testament to the
glorious and extraordinary
merging and transcending of difference,
a testament to peace -which must surely be the kernel
that drives us on.

And if journeys let us stand back – review the world,
let this be a turning point, a brand new year
the city all around us, these pillars,
the mosaic spectacle of tower block,
the city a kaleidoscope, a daring embroidery
spread out like spokes, a web, itself a giant wheel
encompassing, each of us carrying wrapped inside ourselves
our own threads and journeys,
each one of us an infinitesimal part
such that every wrong, tear or break
is ours too,
stitched into the very tapestry of us.